OVERWATCH

KENNY ABDO

Fly!
An Imprint of Abdo Zoom
abdobooks.com

abdobooks.com

Published by Abdo Zoom, a division of ABDO, P.O. Box 398166, Minneapolis, Minnesota 55439. Copyright © 2023 by Abdo Consulting Group, Inc. International copyrights reserved in all countries. No part of this book may be reproduced in any form without written permission from the publisher. Fly!™ is a trademark and logo of Abdo Zoom.

Printed in the United States of America, North Mankato, Minnesota.
052022
092022

Photo Credits: Alamy, Getty Images, Newscom, Shutterstock, ©Reino Game p.cover / CC BY-SA 2.0, ©your salty support p.6/ CC BY-NC-ND 2.0, ©Marco Verch Professional Photographer p.21/ CC BY 2.0

Production Contributors: Kenny Abdo, Jennie Forsberg, Grace Hansen

Design Contributors: Candice Keimig, Neil Klinepier

Library of Congress Control Number: 2021950294

Publisher's Cataloging-in-Publication Data

Names: Abdo, Kenny, author.

Title: Overwatch / by Kenny Abdo.

Description: Minneapolis, Minnesota : Abdo Zoom, 2023 | Series: Esports | Includes online resources and index.

Identifiers: ISBN 9781098228507 (lib. bdg.) | ISBN 9781644947869 (pbk.) | ISBN 9781098229344 (ebook) | ISBN 9781098229764 (Read-to-Me ebook)

Subjects: LCSH: Video games--Juvenile literature. | eSports (Contests)--Juvenile literature. | Overwatch (Video game)--Juvenile literature. | Blizzard Entertainment (Firm)--Juvenile literature. | Imaginary wars and battles--Juvenile literature.

Classification: DDC 794.8--dc23

TABLE OF CONTENTS

OVERWATCH

Coming in hot as one of 2016's best new games, *Overwatch* has set the esport scene on fire!

The game created a unique world filled with **lore** and characters that have connected players around the world!

Video game **developer** Blizzard needed a hit when its biggest game *Titan* was cancelled.

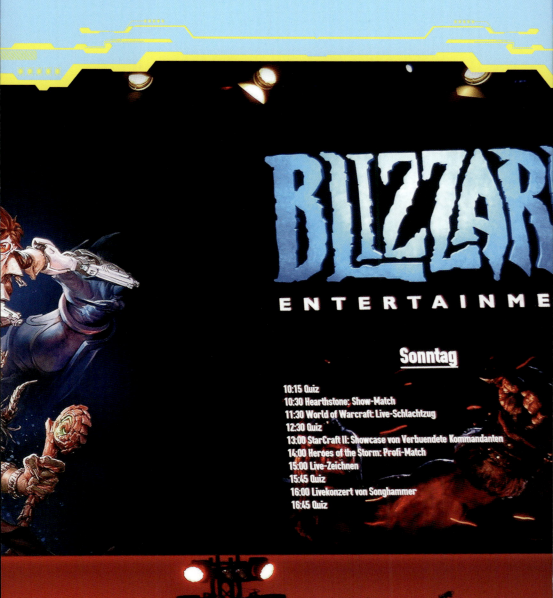

Blizzard's designers came up with a team-based shooter that took many ideas from *Titan*. Eventually, it became *Overwatch*, which was released in 2016.

XBOX ONE

VERWATCH

ORIGINS EDITION

OMEZENÝ BONUS
>> SKIN NOIRE WIDOWMAKER

BLIZZARD
ENTERTAINMENT

VYŽADUJE ZLATÉ ČLENSTVÍ XBOX LIVE

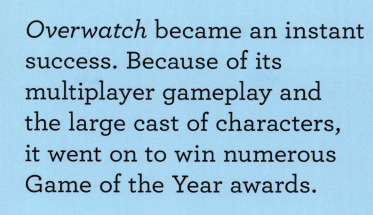

Overwatch became an instant success. Because of its multiplayer gameplay and the large cast of characters, it went on to win numerous Game of the Year awards.

JOURNEY

Blizzard hosts a convention every year called BlizzCon. During the 2016 event, the company announced the arrival of the Overwatch **League** (OWL).

The first **season** of OWL was in 2018. The London Spitfire became the first team to win with a 3-1 victory over the Philadelphia Fusion. The team walked away with $1.4 million!

The San Francisco Shock **swept** the Vancouver Titans in four matches to become the 2019 **season** champions. Choi "ChoiHyoBin" Hyo-bin of the Shock was named the finals **MVP**.

The 2020 **season** was moved to online play due to the COVID-19 **pandemic**. Team San Francisco Shock beat out Seoul Dynasty at the **Grand Finals**!

The 2021 **season** remained mostly online. The Shanghai Dragons clinched their first **championship** against the Atlanta Reign in a limited live event.

Teams participating in the 2022 **season** were some of the first to play *Overwatch 2*. Players got to see new players and gameplay firsthand!

The Overwatch **League** has come a long way since it was first announced at Blizzcon. For fans of the league, there has been a lot to love from the very beginning.

GLOSSARY

championship – a game held to find a first-place winner.

developer – a company that builds and creates software and video games.

Grand Finals – the post-season championship series of the Overwatch League.

league – a group of teams that compete against each other.

lore – a story handed down from person to person.

MVP – short for most valuable player, an award that is given to the best-performing esport athlete.

pandemic – a widespread outbreak of disease that afflicts many people over different continents.

season – the portion of the year when certain games are played.

sweep – when a team wins every event, award, or place in a competition.

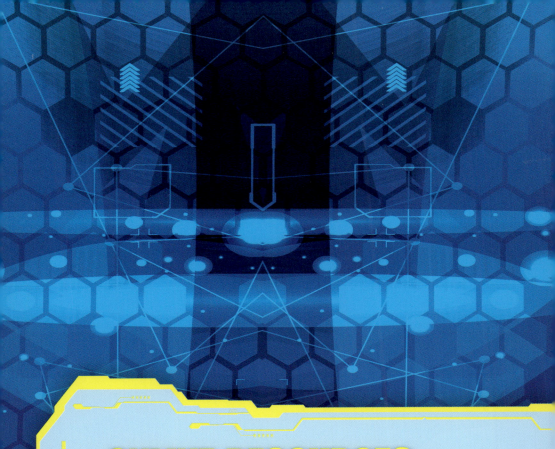

ONLINE RESOURCES

Booklinks
NONFICTION NETWORK
FREE! ONLINE NONFICTION RESOURCES

To learn more about Overwatch, please visit **abdobooklinks.com** or scan this QR code. These links are routinely monitored and updated to provide the most current information available.

INDEX